How To Avoid Legal Pitfalls That Cost Landlords Thousands of Dollars

By Brian Xavier Pendergraft Esq.
Real Estate & Estate Planning Attorney
The Pendergraft Firm, LLC.
www.TPF.legal

"The Landlord That Fails To Plan Plans on Losing Big."

Publisher: Pendergraft Press
ISBN-13: 978-0-9980982-0-3

Disclaimer

This primer provides legal information, not legal advice. For legal advice, the application of law to your individual circumstance, you should consult with a local landlord lawyer.

Special Thanks

Special thanks to my mother, Denise Williams-Brown, for making me so I could make this book.

Table of Contents

Introduction

I am a Maryland and District of Columbia Real Estate and Estate Planning Attorney. I help landlords and real estate investors with their legal needs. This is not the primer I wanted to write, it is the one I needed to write. In many instances, by the time a landlord-tenant case gets to me it has already been decided. If a landlord has fallen into one or more of the pitfalls that I have been mentioned in this book, then chances are I cannot get them the maximum amount of money they believe that they are due, or in some instances any money at all. In the worst case scenario, I have to put on my criminal defense attorney hat to protect landlords from potential criminal violations. I did not get into real estate to be a criminal defense attorney! Landlords that understand best practices and know how to avoid these pitfalls maximize the chances of me having success in court. Better landlords, or as I like to call them, **Planlords**, help me get better results as an attorney! Read this and help me help you!

Planlord - Advanced Estate Planning For Landlords and Investors Facebook Group

Join our Planlord Mastermind Facebook Group when you are ready to go beyond the basics and create generational wealth. Go from landlord to Planlord!

Pitfall One - The Ultimate Mistake! Renting To Bad Tenants (Failure To Screen)

If there is one pitfall landlords need to avoid this is it. The biggest, maximum, ultimate whopper of a mistake that landlords make is renting to bad tenants. A bad tenant is a tenant who (1) does not pay rent and (2) wrecks the place, and you should not rent to these people. As obvious as this sounds apparently it is not obvious. Many landlords rent to tenants without first verifying their ability to pay rent and whether or not they have a good rental history. You can verify whether or not prospective tenants will be good tenants by screening them. **Tenant screening** allows you to find out your prospective tenants income, military status, rental history, criminal history, employment history, eviction history, whether or not they smoke, and whether or not they have pets and so on. After screening your tenants you can deny them for valid reasons such as the inability to pay, poor rental history, relevant criminal record and so on.

There are laws you must comply with when screening tenants including but not limited to the Fair Credit Reporting Act and the Fair and Accurate Credit Transaction Act. So consider consulting with local legal counsel before implementing your tenant screening process, or hiring a reputable property management company to screen your tenants for you. Property management companies often screen tenants at a low cost. Paying to have a tenant screened is a small price to pay in comparison to the thousands of dollars you **will lose** for renting to bad tenants.

Pitfall Two - Failure To Get Rental License and Property Up to Housing Code

A huge mistake landlords make is that they decide they want to rent their property and just go for it. It does not even occur to them that may be breaking the law from the start. Depending on your jurisdiction you may be required to have a rental license in order to rent property. Before renting check with your local residential housing department or with local counsel whether or not your jurisdiction requires for you to have a rental license. In the majority of the jurisdictions I practice in landlords are required to have rental licenses, and if they do not then they are barred from filing for **failure to pay rent**, which is the fastest way to evict tenants and the best way (and more often than not the only way) to get a judgment against a tenant for unpaid rent.

Landlords that fail to ensure that a property is up to housing code not only put themselves at risk for losing money but for at risk of civil and **criminal** citations. I am helping more than one landlord in cases where they are facing criminal and civil citations because of this mistake. Opportunistic tenants whom never intended to pay rent anyway will often use these circumstances to justify the non-payment of rent or to file suit against you for rent escrow. Avoid this pitfall all together and make sure your property is up to local housing code **before renting.** Contact your local residential housing licensing and inspections department for more information on licensing and rental housing code requirements.

Pitfall Three - Using Oral Lease Agreements

Landlords often use oral lease agreements. In many jurisdictions, landlords are unable to recover unpaid rent if they do not have written lease agreements. Even if your rental property is on the moon and a **written lease agreement** is not required, it is still a best practice to have one because without it your lease is your word against your tenants. A written lease agreement says who pays for utilities, how much the rent is, whether or not smoking or pets are allowed, and so on.

Surprisingly often, a written lease agreement is a landlord's best form of protection from liability. For example, many tenants often try to sue landlords for property damage due to unforeseen circumstances out of their landlord's control. One time a tenant called me because a fire was caused by another tenant who stuck something flammable in a microwave which caused a fire that destroyed her personal property. She wanted to sue her landlord to hold him responsible for replacing her damaged property. Her lease agreement made her responsible for getting her own rental property insurance and replacing her damaged property. This discouraged an experienced landlord-tenant attorney (myself) from filing suit against the landlord. A landlord is much more vulnerable without the protection of a well-written lease agreement.

Pitfall Four - Using Illegal Lease Agreements

It's not enough to use a written lease agreement. Use a written lease agreement that complies with you Local, State, and Federal law. If you use a lease agreement with illegal provisions, in the best case scenario, a court will simply not enforce the illegal provisions. In the worst case scenario a landlord can face heavy sanctions.

For example, I once had to redraft a lease agreements for a landlord after the Maryland Consumer Protection Division heavily sanctioned them for using leases that they found were illegal, against public policy, and fraudulent. These particular leases contained provisions that (1) charged late fees higher than the legal rate (2) limited landlord's liability in ALL situations (3) leased the property "as is" (3) made tenant responsible for ALL repairs (4) waived tenants right to sue for ANY reason (4) a non-refundable security deposit (5) placed a lien on tenants property upon default. These provisions are essentially the exact *opposite* of what is allowed to be in a lease agreement where I practice. Be sure that your lease agreement complies with local, State, and Federal law. Consider consulting with a local lawyer to draft or review your lease agreements.

In my experience many leases found online and many local standard forms have illegal lease provisions. An experienced landlord-tenant attorney can review your leases for legal sufficiency.

Pitfall Five - Bad (or no) Financial Record Keeping

The better your records the better your chances of getting your desired outcome in court. Landlord-Tenant Court is often jam packed and Judges are trying to get through the high volume of cases that they need to hear that day and they may not give your case the attention that it needs. A conventional **rent ledger** that tracks a tenants payment history goes a very long way in landlord-tenant court. A Judge can look at one and quickly determine how much money to award you, they have seen thousands of them. You can find sample rent ledgers online or you can contact me and I will be happy to send you a sample one.

In many jurisdictions landlords are required to track the date, the amount, and by whom rent money was paid. For example if I am representing a tenant in Maryland landlord-tenant court and if a landlord cannot produce financial records, I will ask the Court to dismiss the case and quote the statute that requires landlords to keep such records, and it most likely will be dismissed. Avoid this problem by keeping accurate records.

Pitfall Six - Failure To Give Tenants Receipts

Your jurisdiction may require you to give tenants receipts when they make payments. Many jurisdictions require that receipts are given every time a tenant makes a payment using **cash.** These receipts will protect you in the event there is a dispute over payment. In the worst case scenario, I have seen a District Court Judge throw out a failure to pay rent case because the landlord did not give the tenant required receipts. Do not let this be you! Carbonless copy receipt books are about $5 on Amazon. $5 now could save you $5000 later! Check your jurisdictions local laws to determine under what circumstances you are required to give receipts.

Pitfall Seven - No Initial Walkthrough, or Inadequate Walkthrough

It is very common for tenants to claim property damage was caused prior to their rental. An initial walkthrough done correctly can protect you in the event you and your tenant have a dispute over who caused what damages. A great way to do a walkthrough is to use a thorough checklist of the property's fixtures and assets. Standard initial walkthrough forms can be purchased. Both landlord and tenant should go through the form together and both sign off on the condition of the property before the tenant rents. In many jurisdictions, a walkthrough is required if the landlord wants to take a security deposit.

I think it is a great idea to **take pictures** of the property in the tenant's presence, and for both landlord and tenant to sign and date the back of the photos. These photos can be great evidence in the event tenant damages the property and tries to claim the damages were caused before he or she rented. Be sure to provide the tenant copies of the photos if you do this.

Pitfall Eight - Discrimination, and Not So Obvious Discrimination

The **Fair Housing Act** makes it illegal for landlords to refuse to rent on the basis of race, skin color, national origin, religion, gender, familial status, and disability. Some forms of discrimination are obvious such as refusing to rent to a family based on their color, but some forms are less obvious. A landlord contacted me because she wanted to evict a tenant because she was allegedly having intercourse with her boyfriend on the property and it was against her religious beliefs. *This is not legal.* Unmarried couples cannot be discriminated against, just like married or gay couples.

Landlords have to be careful that their advertising for rentals does not run afoul of the Fair Housing Act. Avoid using pictures of people in your marketing because it can be perceived as discriminatory against groups of people not represented in the photo. Specifically advertising to any group (men only, women only, whites only, blacks only etc.) or excluding groups (no transsexuals allowed, no families allowed, etc.) should be avoided. There are some exceptions to the Fair Housing Act such as Senior Housing, so discrimination is allowed in certain circumstances. If you do wish to provide housing to only a specific group of people, review the Fair Housing Act and consult with an attorney. Landlords found liable for Housing Discrimination have **lost multi-million dollar law suits.**

Pitfall Nine - Not Knowing How To Handle Security Deposits

Security deposit rules vary greatly from State to State. Generally your jurisdiction tells you (1) the maximum amount you're allowed to charge (2) whether or not it must be stored in a separate bank account for security deposits (3) when it can be used (4) how to properly withhold the security deposit (5) and whether or not it must be returned with interest, and if so how much (6) and whether or not a pet deposit is treated as a security deposit. Failure to follow your jurisdiction's rules could result in the forfeiture of your right to use the security deposit. For example in Maryland, a landlord must send the tenant a letter within 45 days of the end of the tenancy detailing how the security deposit was used. If she does not, then she forfeits the right to use the security deposit *even if* the tenant did in fact cause damages. Security deposit misuse in Maryland could subject a landlord to three times the amount of the security deposit, and reasonable attorneys fees. Make sure you follow your jurisdiction's rules if you intend to take security deposits.

Pitfall Ten - Not Knowing Your Obligations As A Landlord

At the very least, as a landlord you owe your client a duty to ensure that the property is fit for habitation, not dangerous, and to do maintenance and repairs for structural issues. Many residential landlords just rent to tenants and expect the tenants to take care of everything. *As a general rule this is not legal.* There may be issues that affect the habitability of a property that a landlord must fix, even if landlord believes that the tenant caused the issue. If these issues are not remedied the landlord subjects himself to failing a code enforcement inspection and facing a civil or criminal penalties. The tenant could also attempt to exercise any remedies that may be available to him or her under law.

Not knowing your obligations as a landlord could have severe penalties. Consider consulting with a local attorney if you have any questions about your obligations to your tenants.

Pitfall Eleven - Poor or Inadequately Done Final Walkthrough

The final walkthrough should be done with a checklist similarly to the initial walkthrough. The mistake landlords make is when they try to hold the tenant liable for damages that they find *after* the final walkthrough. Days after the final walkthrough the landlord will discover that the dishwasher does not work and try to bill the tenant for it. This is not a best practice. The purpose of the final walkthrough is so that the tenant can be present for the final inspection, and citing your tenant for any damages you find afterward defeats the purpose of the final inspection. You should discover the damages during the final walkthrough in the tenant's presence, so be thorough and inspect everything!

Pitfall Twelve - "Self Help" Evictions

Evicting residential tenants or even squatters without a court order is probably a **crime** in most jurisdictions. It definitely is in mine. Do not do it otherwise you could face civil or criminal penalties.

"Constructive" eviction occurs when a landlord tries to get a tenant to leave by decreasing services or otherwise treating their tenants badly.

It's called "constructive" because technically the tenant left on their own volition and not against their will like a standard eviction. However constructive eviction is treated the same as a standard illegal eviction.

Some examples of constructive eviction include cutting off utilities, refusing to fix substantial habitability issues on the property, or threatening the tenant with violence.

Residential landlords should go through their local landlord-tenant court to evict tenants and not take the law into their own hands. **Changing the locks** is an eviction! Review your jurisdictions applicable eviction laws or consult with an eviction lawyer before attempting to evict tenants or squatters.

Pitfall Thirteen - "Retaliatory" Action

Retaliatory Action is a defense that is available against landlords in many jurisdictions when a landlord takes "adverse action" against a tenant after a tenant has exercised a legal right including but not limited to: (1) complaining about unsafe or illegal living conditions to the landlord (2) reporting landlord to a government agency or (3) joining or organizing a tenant's rights organizations.

Adverse action may vary from jurisdiction to jurisdiction, but here are some examples: (1) trying to evict or "constructive evict" tenant (2) increasing rent (3) decreasing services (4) or refusing to renew a lease.

The damages for retaliatory action can be very high depending on your jurisdiction. In Maryland, a tenant can be awarded up three months rent, reasonable attorney's fees, and court costs.

To prevent yourself from falling into this pitfall, be sure to keep a written record of correspondence with your tenants especially if your landlord-tenant relationship starts to get hostile. You need to be able to show that you are evicting your tenant for the right reasons, and not for revenge.

Pitfall Fourteen - Legal Action Without First Consulting With An Attorney

At the very least consider **consulting** with an attorney before court proceedings because I can almost guarantee you that your tenants are. I get daily phone calls from non-paying tenants that cannot afford to pay you, and have no way of paying me, but are looking for any "loophole" they can find to not pay you rent and stay on your property. "Tenant friendly" (read landlord-deadly) jurisdictions such as Washington, DC have a culture that favors tenants and tenants are they are often represented by solid pro-bono attorneys. The **system in and of itself** is a pitfall designed to stack the deck against landlords. In such jurisdictions, having an attorney that has worked within that system can be very helpful to you.

Landlords with multiple tenants can generally reduce attorneys fees by working out deals with a law office to handle all of their filings. In addition, a landlord's liability insurance may cover attorney's fees in the event they are sued by a tenant.

Pitfall Fifteen - Leaving Money On The Table

So you went to court and you won multiple judgments against tenants and you do not have the time or the know how to collect judgments. Consider consulting with an attorney to collect your judgments on your behalf. Attorneys generally on an hourly or contingency fee basis, however, if you have multiple cases you can often work out a better rate.

Judgments can be enforce by garnishing the tenants bank account, wages, and other assets. Other tools in the toolbox are credit reporting or filing a lien against the tenant.

A judgment without enforcement is just a piece of paper, so start enforcing! You can also consider using a collection agency.

Bonus One - Always Make Monthly Rent Due on The First

Please make my job and the courts job easier by always making rent due on the **first.** Many landlords make rent due on the same day that the tenant moves in. If your tenant does not move in on the first, I think it is a best practice to **pro-rate** the rent for the first month and start with the normal monthly rent on the first of the next month.

Courts are accustomed to seeing rent due on the first. Landlord-Tenant court dockets for failure to pay rent cases revolve around rent being due the first and attorneys filing as soon as they are legally allowed to do so after the first.

Rent always being due the first is also a great business practice for building your real estate empire. You will always know when your money is due!

Bonus Two - Business Law Basics - Legal and Insurance

At a minimum I recommend forming a **business entity** and obtaining **liability insurance** to just about anyone looking to start a business. A business entity protects you by creating a hurdle between you and people who want to hold you personally liable. Liability insurance can protect you if you end up in a lawsuit. Landlord's can specifically get **landlord insurance** that can cover legal fees or lost rental income. I know many landlords that have lost tens of thousands of dollars that could have greatly benefitted from landlord insurance.

For investors looking to invest in real estate together, a **joint venture** agreement that covers importation topics such as the purpose of the venture, ownership and management, the legal framework, the duty of loyalty, and exit strategies. In a perfect world, each investor will have his or her own attorney when negotiating the deal. One attorney can do the deal if the investors are willing to sign waivers. Anything is better than no attorney.

I think it's best for anyone who wants to know what type of entity (LLC vs. S-Corp vs. Corporation) they should form for their business should consult with a real estate attorney for liability advice, and a real estate CPA for tax advice. Then you will be able to determine which entity best suits your individual needs.

Bonus Three - Property Management Considerations

A property manager can help you by navigating all the pitfalls mentioned in this book (and more) for you. Property managers can find tenants, screen tenants, rent property, do maintenance, and correspond with the tenants for you. Property managers generally cost between 8%-10% of the monthly rent. Good property managers know how to comply with local, State, Federal laws and follow landlord best practices so you do not have to worry about that stuff. You do not have to use a property manager, but at least consider it. It may be worth the peace of mind knowing you have professionals on the job.

If you do decide to use a property manger then understand that you as the property owner have a **"principal-agent"** relationship with your property management company. As principal, you are liable for your agents misconduct.

You cannot just blindly trust your property manager to take care of everything. I have assisted landlords in going after their property management company for failing to monitor and manage the property as promised, resulting in significant losses to the landlord. Do your due diligence to find and hire the best property managers to avoid this pitfall.

Bonus Four - Planlord - Advanced Estate Planning For Landlords and Investors Facebook Group

In order to truly ascend from a landlord to a Planlord, estate planning and asset protection strategies must be used to protect your assets. The complexity of such strategies are beyond the scope of this primer. Clever use of business entities in conjunction with land trusts and insurance, can greatly **minimize the risk** that comes with owning property and help create **generational wealth.**

As landlords and investors, you are a **targets** for lawsuits. The last thing you want is for the real estate empire you've worked to build your entire life to be taken from you. This is a very real risk for those who do not plan correctly.

I created the mastermind Facebook group **Planlord - Advanced Estate Planning for Landlords and Investors**, to discuss the best asset protection and strategies with estate planners, landlords, real estate investors, and certified public accountants.

We welcome the smallest landlords to the largest real estate tycoons to join us! You can find the group by searching for "Planlord" in the Facebook search bar. It is a closed group so I will have to approve you to join. Feel free to shoot me an e-mail at info@tpf.legal if I am taking too long to approve you!

Resources For Landlords

Landlordology.com - Practical landlord guides and State laws and regulations.

MrLandlord.com - Has a huge amount of resources for landlords.

BiggerPockets.com - Very popular forum for real estate investors. They have a forum for landlord Q & A where landlords help each other out. They also have an informative podcast on real estate investing!

Avvo.com - Can be used to ask questions to local landlord-tenant lawyers. If your question concerns property located in DC or MD, there is a good chance you'll get an answer from me!

TPF.legal - My website! I try to regularly add content for landlords and real estate investors. **Planlord.com** is still under construction at the time of the release of this primer.

Nolo.com - For "Do it yourself" legal products and helpful books.

Your local landlord tenant help center - You jurisdiction may have a local help center you can visit to ask questions.

Your local REIA (Real Estate Investors Association) probably has landlords that are willing to help you.

About Me

I, Brian Xavier Pendergraft, am a real estate and estate planning attorney and my practice primarily consists of turning landlords and real estate investors into Planlords by helping them create and maintain generational wealth. I am licensed to practice law in both Maryland and the District of Columbia. Feel free to contact me if you have any questions!

Phone: 301-200-0777

Email: info@tpf.legal

Website: www.TPF.legal

Facebook: facebook.com/pendergraftfirm

Google+: google.com/+pendergraftfirm

Twitter: twitter.com/pendergraftfirm

Twitter: twitter.com/planlord

Reviews and More From Me

Please visit **www.booksbybrian.com** to be linked to my amazon page for my book offerings where you can leave me a review. This is the only book there now, but with your support I can write many more!

Made in the USA
Monee, IL
05 November 2026

67377170R00016